There are two main purposes in writing this book for independent musicians, artists managers and record labels...

Firstly, so that you get **results as quickly as possible** and grow your next 1,000 superfans faster than ever before.

But secondly and more practically, **I want to work closely with you** for months and years to come and be by your side defining your content strategy, planning your single releases and teaching you **everything** I know about social media.

To do that however, we need to **unlearn** everything the music industry has ever taught you about social media.

Wait - what's wrong with the way you promote your music right now? Be honest and tell me if this sounds familiar...

1) You get excited and announce new music is coming soon.
2) You shout about the release date and link in bio.
3) You get depressed at the number of likes, views, streams and end up slowing down on the posting.
4) You retreat into "ghost mode" until your next release.

See how selfish that sounds? It's all about **YOU** - not the **listener**.

We need to **replace promotion with emotion** and take them on a journey through what you experienced and unlock some similar part of them that **feels the same.**

My goal is to build your mindset **WHY** you need to create content, **WHAT** you're going to say or do, **HOW** to make it look exciting and **WHERE** to post it!

Are you ready??

In writing this ebook I went and bought or signed up for nearly every single PDF, course or resource from the world of social media marketers for musicians...and do you know what I realised?

NOBODY is sharing the real truth about how to grow a fanbase as an artist or practical steps to promote a single. Everything felt like they were saving the best tips for themselves without sharing the real deal that moves the needle.

I read checklists and strategies saying:

1. **Submit to playlists**
2. **Contact influencers**
3. **Build a content calendar**
4. **Make a contacts list**

No shit! That's a good idea without a plan. But the <u>real</u> question is **HOW?**

The first stumbling block every musician faces is **WHERE** do I start?

I want to give you the reasoning, the ideas, the execution and the inspiration to enjoy this part of your journey.

Every single one of us enjoy making music right? It's what we love. So the goal is to make **creating content and promoting the music** feel as euphoric as the creation process itself!

Get ready! You're going to learn social media like you learnt how to ride a bicycle **- with your training wheels on!** Together we'll push the boundaries until you'll learn how to fly solo.

Let's get started with your training...

Ayaz Aftab Hussain

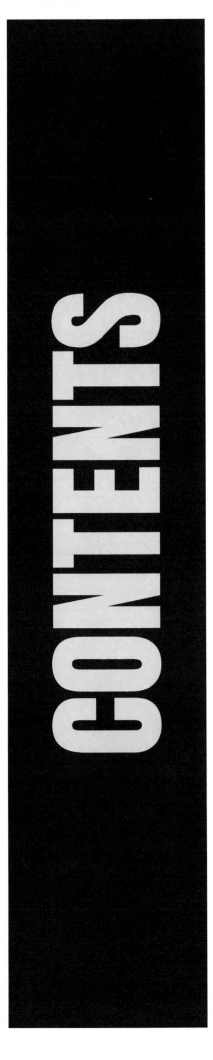

CONTENTS

TWO TYPES **OF** FANS

SECRET SOCIAL MEDIA PLAYBOOK

04 **CHAPTER ONE**
How American Football Changed My Life

10 **CHAPTER TWO**
Finding Your X's

21 **CHAPTER THREE**
Finding Your O's

38 **CHAPTER FOUR**
Creating Unignorable Content

42 **CHAPTER FIVE**
Your New Social Media Strategy

48 **CHAPTER SIX**
Duplicate Then Stagger

TWOTYPESOFFANS.COM

CHAPTER ONE:
AMERICAN FOOTBALL CHANGED MY LIFE

I discovered the incredible sport of American Football at university and surprisingly it taught me a life changing lesson about music marketing.

On a cold wintery night in the student union, the 2010 Super Bowl was playing on the big projector screen. I'll never forget the matchup of the New Orleans Saints Vs the Indianapolis Colts.

I had zero idea what was happening until some friends suggested teaching me the rules with a drinking game.

They laughed at my misery while making a repulsive mocktail of Pepsi, salt, pepper, mustard, vinegar, mayonnaise, Tabasco, horseradish sauce and ketchup... then forced me to take a sip every time something eventful happened!

No word of a lie, I threw up because of the drink but fell in love with the sport! The very next day, I was dragged along to American Football training to try out for the university sports team.

It was unbelievably confusing and to this day, I've never forgotten how the coaches used to draw up diagrams with complex tactics for catching, running and blocking.

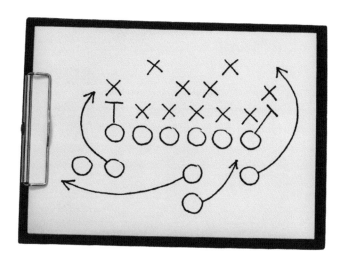

IN THE DIAGRAMS, THERE WERE TWO DIFFERENT SYMBOLS X'S AND O'S.

YOUR OPPONENTS

X's are other **musicians** who <u>create</u> similar style music to you.

YOUR TEAM

O's are **listeners** who <u>enjoy</u> similar styles of music to you.

During one particularly wet and cold weekly practice, the Coach could see I was struggling with a simple blocking assignment (despite being the tallest player on the entire team).

With a look of confusion from the diagrams, he called me aside after the team huddle for a lesson that stuck with me forever.

> ## "YOU CAN ONLY TACKLE ONE PERSON AT A TIME.
>
> ## WHEN THE WHISTLE BLOWS, LASER FOCUS YOUR EFFORT AND HIT THAT PERSON HARD."

This fundamental thought sparked the idea for my model **The Two Types Of Fans: X's and O's.**

I started to wonder if you could create DIFFERENT types of content for DIFFERENT types of fans.

Over several years I ran A/B split tests to experiment how to target **musician audiences versus fan audiences**, by using alternative titles, images, platforms and channels.

X's ARE OTHER MUSICIANS

O's ARE THE FANS

TWOTYPESOFFANS.COM

DO YOU NEED TO PICK AND ONLY TARGET X'S OR O'S?

No! You don't need to pick between the two types of fans, let me paint you a picture why you might want to.

Most artists probably want to target **BOTH X's and O's** but depending on your objective as an artist, there are a few use cases where you might want to pick only one of the two groups.

ONLY TARGETING X'S

If you were a producer selling sample packs, it wouldn't be useful at all to only target O's.

Fans don't buy the musician specific product you are selling.

Instead of Business2Business (B2B) selling, think of this as a Musician2Musician (M2M) sales strategy to target X's!

ONLY TARGETING O'S

If you want to sell t-shirts and merchandise, you may want to avoid targeting X's.

Let's be honest, **musicians rarely wear merch from their rival musicians to advertise them** (unless they are a gift or really close friends).

So if your target audience are fans of your music, focus on O's only.

TARGETING X'S AND O'S

If you want to attract more gigs, you'll need target **both fans and Club Promoters, Booking Agents and industry contacts** (yes, the music industry can be categorised as an extension of X's).

Targeting O's proves you can sell tickets or have a buzz around your music but engaging with X's such as the venue manager gets the attention of the decision makers will ultimately book you for gigs and shows.

CHAPTER TWO:
FINDING YOUR X'S

Whenever I connect with artists, managers or record labels in social media workshops, I can almost guarantee their first question will be: **"WHAT content should we be posting about?"**

With a cheeky grin, I ask a counter-question: "the more important question is **WHO are we creating content for?"**

The whole point of this method is to think of your audience as two different streams of **X's and O's.**

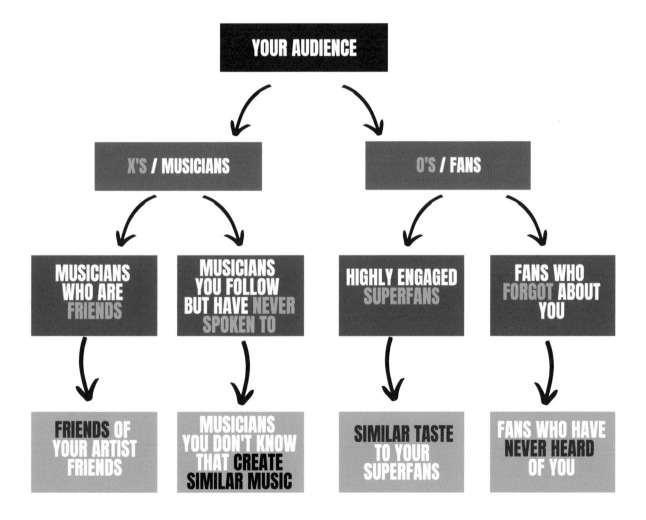

As you can see, there are 8 virtually undiscovered audiences that you aren't tapping into properly. That's fundamentally why you find it so hard to grow on social media, because you're sharing what YOU want to post and not what your fans WANT to see.

Let's tackle half the diagram to specifically **target other musicians.**

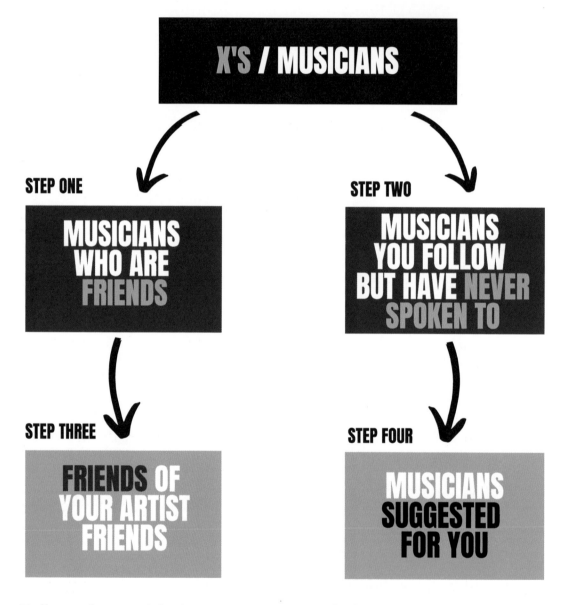

Follow along with the upcoming **worksheets** on Page 12 or replicate your own table in the Notes section of your phone or with a good old fashioned piece of paper and pen!

WORKSHEET #1

RELATES TO STEP ONE AND STEP TWO FROM PAGE 12 AND 13

Musicians Friends Username or URL	**Never Spoken To** Username or URL

STEP ONE - MUSICIANS WHO ARE FRIENDS

a) Start by opening Instagram, Facebook, Twitter or any other platform and open the list of people **Who You Follow** or your **Friends List.**

b) Scroll down the **Following** list to the bottom until you reach the first users you ever followed after launching your account. On Instagram there is a shortcut to **Sort by Date followed: Earliest** to make this quicker!

c) In the first worksheet column, **write down the usernames of all the musicians you are friends with**. (By "friends", I mean you've chatted to them on DMs before or physically met.)

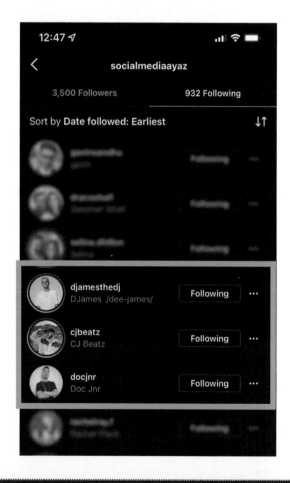
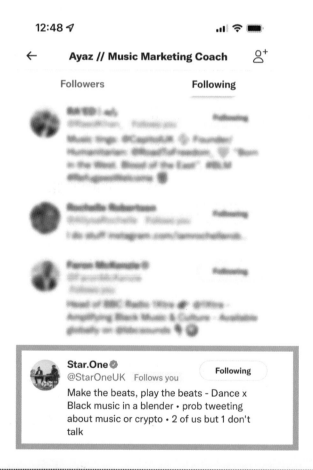

STEP TWO - MUSICIANS YOU HAVE NEVER SPOKEN TO

Move to the second column and make a list of any artists who you recognise but have **never spoken to or interacted with** in the DMs. These are the X's whose attention we need to attract.

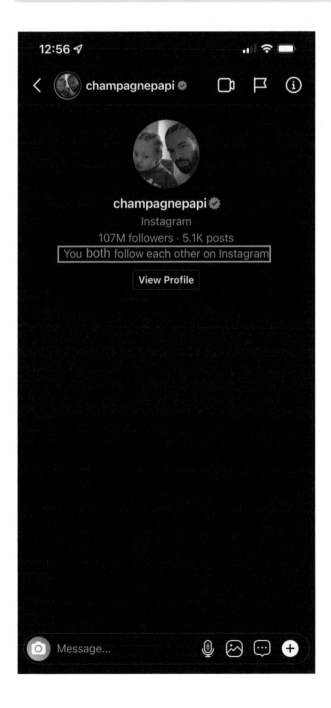

In this imaginary example, you can see both Drake and the user **follow each other but have never spoken in direct messages** or tagged any Stories together.

WORKSHEET #2

RELATES TO STEP THREE AND STEP FOUR FROM PAGE 15 AND 16

Musician Friend Username or URL	Similar Sized Fanbase Username or URL

Consistent Commenters Username or URL	Suggested For You Username or URL

STEP THREE - FRIENDS OF YOUR MUSICIAN FRIENDS

Pick <u>one musician friend</u> from **column one** with whom you have a close relationship and visit their Profile**.**

Scroll down to examine their **most recent posts** and look for patterns of **recurring names who are consistently liking their posts or commenting.**

Write down the usernames of these friends of your musicians friends who **you do not know.**

These are the X's you **want to attract.**

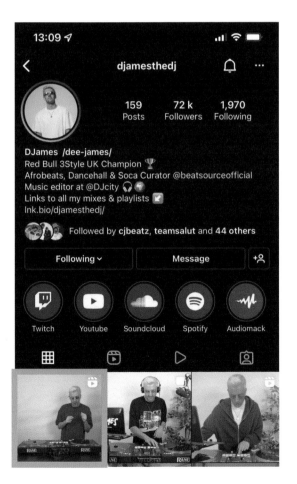

STEP FOUR - MUSICIANS SUGGESTED FOR YOU

The next step is to pick <u>one musician friend</u> who has a **similar number of fans** to you and head to their Profile.

You will see either a small arrow next or a person icon with a plus sign which opens up the **Suggested For You list.**

The musicians shown here are being detected by algorithm to be similar artists you don't know yet.

Write down some of these usernames in the column of **Musicians Suggested For You** in the next worksheet.

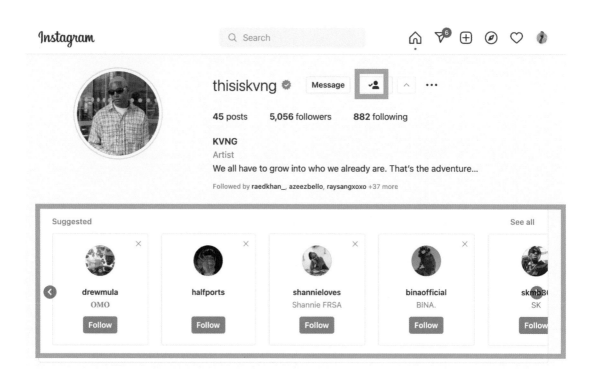

WELL DONE FOR MAKING
YOUR LISTS...BUT WAIT!!

IT'S VERY IMPORTANT THAT YOU
<u>DON'T</u> START FOLLOWING ALL
OF THESE NEW PEOPLE YET...

YOUR PROFILE ISN'T OPTIMISED YET
WITH THE TYPE OF CONTENT YOU
NEED TO CREATE IN ORDER TO
ATTRACT THOSE OTHER MUSICIANS
BACK TO YOUR ACCOUNT.

FINDING YOUR X'S - STRATEGY EXPLANATION

GROUP ONE - EXISTING MUSICIAN FRIENDS

Targeting our existing musician friends helps us develop a **baseline or minimum level of engagement** because we already know the interests of this audience already.

GROUP TWO - MUSICIANS WE HAVE NEVER SPOKEN TO

Remember, these musicians <u>already follow you</u>, but since you have never spoken, we need to catch their attention. By making your **content unignorable**, you start to catch the attention of artists who have never heard of you.

GROUP THREE - FRIENDS OF YOUR MUSICIANS FRIENDS

This group of people are <u>already connected </u>with your friends so we need steal the spotlight. By making your posts **irresistibly shareable onto people's Stories** their audience will begin to discover who you are and the content you create.

GROUP FOUR - MUSICIANS SUGGESTED FOR YOU

Being aware of the musicians that the algorithm is detecting you are similar to is important. As more musicians interact with your content, YOU will be **shown to others** as a suggestion for a user they should follow.

AS YOU CREATE CONTENT THAT IS UNIGNORABLE...

YOU BEGIN TO CATCH THE ATTENTION OF ARTISTS WHO HAVE NEVER HEARD OF YOU

CHAPTER THREE:
FINDING YOUR O'S

It's time to talk about your fans. If I asked you off the bat,
"how many fans do you have?"

Would your first instinct be to count how many <u>followers</u> you have across Instagram, Facebook, Twitter and maybe Soundcloud?

Let's be clear though, **followers are not fans!** There is a monumental difference between having subscribers and having a fanbase.

Followers or Subscribers are people who <u>opt-in</u> to be shown future previews of your content; but it <u>does not</u> mean they interact with them.

Fans care deeply about every move you make to listen, watch, discuss and interact with you in both a digital and physical landscape.

At an extreme level your superfans will want to:

- **buy tickets to your shows** (just for the chance to see you)
- **grab your merchandise** (to show how much they love you)
- **comment on your posts** (in case you comment back)
- **join your livestreams** (so you can say their name)
- **share your music** (to tell others they heard about you first)

So let me ask you again...

HOW MANY FANS DO YOU HAVE?

There are so many different nuances to the term "fans" that we need to break up the audience into smaller segments to understand **how to create content that satisfies their needs.**

My philosophy is that a fanbase is made up of two segments:

- **active followers** who engage with your content
- **passive followers** who are aware of your posts but are not motivated enough to engage.

If you feel your fanbase is made up of **existing friends and family** rather than the perfect listeners of your music, the exercise in this section will be perfect for you.

Back in 2008, Wired Magazine editor Kevin Kelly wrote an essay entitled *'1,000 True Fans'* where he had a theory that for any artist, musician or creative to make a $100,000 living off their art, they simply need 1,000 fans paying $100 per year.

In my head, $100,000 a year salary sounds life-changing, but other experts such as Li Jin supposed that only 100 True Fans were needed each paying $1,000 a year to achieve the same result.

Let's ignore the financial aspect for a moment and only focus on **audience attention.**

OUT OF ALL YOUR FOLLOWERS, DO YOU HAVE AT LEAST 100 TRUE FANS?

In this upcoming worksheet on page 24, I want you to follow 3 steps to describe the traits and characteristics of your **perfect fan.**

Feel free to follow along with the upcoming **worksheet** or continue working with whichever method served you best for the previous exercises.

STEP ONE - FAVOURITE ARTISTS
a) Write down a list of other musicians your perfect customer would listen to.

Imagine this exercise from the perspective of a fan, and think **"other than myself, who else are <u>their</u> favourite artists?"**

Be careful, this is <u>not</u> an exercise into which other artists <u>you</u> like or <u>who you think</u> you are sonically similar to.

Focus on **what your fans enjoys first** and foremost. If it helps, think about opening up a fan's Spotify saved songs, Soundcloud favourites, or YouTube history and ask yourself **"which other artists would be in their library besides my music?"**

WORKSHEET #3

RELATES TO STEP ONE FROM PAGE 22

Artists Your Perfect Fan Also Loves
Username or URL

STEP TWO - FAVOURITE CHANNELS AND INFLUENCERS

b) Write down a list of other Instagram / YouTube / accounts influencers or brand channels your perfect customer would follow.

This is more detailed than the artists they follow, think about platforms like COLORS / TinyDesk NPR / specific radio presenters or hosts that **represent your genre.**

Even though we are focusing on the perfect fan, this is still <u>your list!</u> Don't feel any pressure to write down anything you are "supposed to" if you have never listened to that platform.

If you don't personally listen to *The Joe Rogan Experience Podcast*, triple check that your fans do and you are not writing down any wild assumptions. Including a name on your list that is irrelevant, won't serve you well. Make everything is hyper-relevant to your target audience.

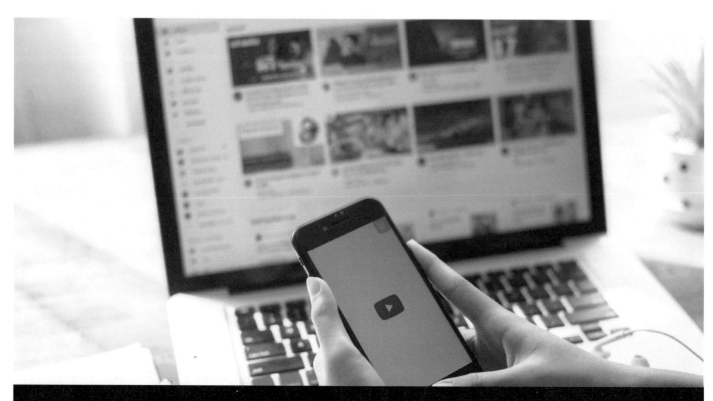

RELATES TO STEP TWO FROM PAGE 25

| **Favourite Channels or Influencers** |
Username or URL

STEP THREE - FAVOURITE CLOTHING BRANDS

c) In the final column, write down the brand names of clothing companies or stores that your perfect customer would typically obsess with.

For example OFF-WHITE clothing or Urban Outfitters might be your go-to places that **create aspiration for where you want to buy clothes.**

Pick carefully and dive deeper than picking obvious brands like Nike and Adidas; unless it's closely related with your audience.

I know this part of the exercise has very little to do with music, but it's one of the most powerful parts of the equation and I can't wait for the mic drop in a minute when you understand how this all comes together...

WORKSHEET #5

RELATES TO STEP THREE FROM PAGE 27

| **Brands That Your Fans Buy** |
Username or URL

WORKSHEET #6

Put your three columns from Worksheet 3, 4 and 5 side by side to begin this exercise.

Imagine realising your perfect fan loved:

- Snoh Aalega and Jorja Smith's music
- BBC 1Xtra and The Breakfast Club interviews
- Stussy and ASOS clothing.

By knowing their passions can you connect with the fans better?

Artists Your Perfect Fans Likes	Presenters / Channels Your Perfect Fan Likes	Clothing Your Perfect Fans Likes

What if...you could mould <u>all</u> of these interests into one or two people? Start by visualising their passions as one or two personas.

Give your top fans made up names and ask yourself: **"will these characters like every single post you create?"**

Imagine as much detail as you can about this perfect superfan including what they do in their free time or what they do for a job.

HELPFUL TIPS

- **What is their name?** Visualise their names realistically to reflect someone in your target audience by considering their ethnicity, age and more! (Don't just pick John and Jane!)

- **How old are they?** Ideally, select a **4 year age spread** e.g 30-34 and consider making your superfans 1 and 2 slightly different ages for an added bonus.

- **Where do they live?** Think carefully and select cities beyond where you live or already have fans. If you can, choose vastly different cities such as Manchester and Los Angeles to give you two completely unique personas.

- **What do they do for fun?** Do they go raving on the weekends or smoke weed recreationally? Be honest about their habits so you can understand their motives.

- **What are their professions?** Knowing if your audience is made up of students, catering and hospitality staff or any other segments helps you know what time of day these audiences are most able to check their phones.

WORKSHEET #7

**Complete the questions from Page 30
and describe your two superfans**

Superfan 1	Superfan 2
Name:	**Name:**
Gender Indentity:	**Gender Indentity:**
Age Range:	**Age Range:**
City:	**City:**
Profession:	**Profession:**
Hobbies:	**Hobbies:**

To finish this exercise, search on Google or Instagram to find a photo of a person that represents the **gender identity, age and ethnicity of your perfect fan.**

Either save these images to your phone or print them out and keep their faces pinned up so you can visualise your superfans everyday.

GIVE YOUR TOP SUPERFANS MADE UP NAMES

WILL THESE CHARACTERS LIKE EVERY SINGLE POST YOU CREATE?

I hope this exercise helps you understand your **perfect superfans** with a new level of clarity.

Because of this short little exercise, you can learn infinite amounts about **how to communicate with your fans.** By knowing what they listen to and what they spend money on, you secretly unlock:

FINDING YOUR O'S - STRATEGY EXPLANATION

GROUP ONE - YOUR PERFECT FAN'S FAVOURITE ARTISTS

Build a cult following by reverse engineering the strategy that made each of these renowned musicians successful. Take the best bits of strategy that Justin Bieber, Travis Scott, Megan Thee Stallion and others used to explode their superfans into obsession.

GROUP TWO - YOUR PERFECT FAN'S FAVOURITE CHANNELS

Build your hitlist of the dream tastemakers who you urgently need to find contacts at. Visualise getting a major co-sign (and the cool factor) for getting played on channels that your audience pay attention to daily!

GROUP THREE - YOUR PERFECT FAN'S FAVOURITE BRANDS

Congratulations, you just made a list of your ideal brand sponsors! Think about the outfit choices for your content, music videos or even clubs you want to play at. Are you ready to style your brand around this framework?

NOW WE KNOW WHAT OUR SUPERFANS LOOK LIKE,

LET'S <u>FIND</u> SOME OF THEM ONLINE...

WHAT CHANNELS DO THEY USE?
WHAT ACCOUNTS DO THEY FOLLOW?
WHAT CONTENT DO THEY WANT TO SEE?

I hope this exercise helps you understand your **perfect superfans** with a new level of clarity.

Doing this exact exercise in consulting workshops with independent musicians is powerful because they start to understand the interests and attractions a fan looks for. Then you can begin to communicate and create in a way that speaks to these superfans.

Now we know what our superfans look like, let's find some of them online...

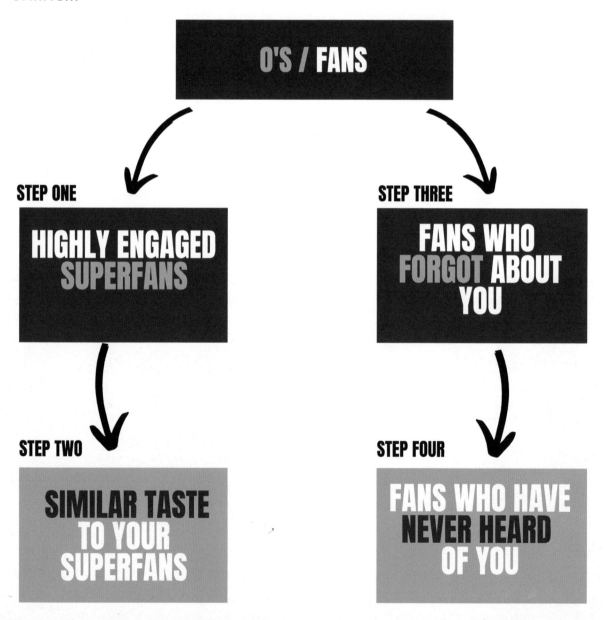

STEP ONE - HIGHLY ENGAGED SUPERFANS

Imagine you've just made a post on Instagram, Twitter or Facebook, **who is usually the first user to Like the post?** Can you think of their name immediately? These are your **highly engaged superfans.**

I'm extremely lucky to have built up great friendships with Benny Bizzie and Kelly Dante who are my highly engaged superfans. I often send them pre-release copies of new social media strategies to ask for their feedback and constructive criticism.

@BENNYBIZZIE   @KELLYDANTEMUSIC

As you get to know your highly engaged superfans, treat them well and <u>never</u> break a promise to them. These are the people who want to **buy** merchandise, concert tickets, NFTs, limited edition vinyl and more from you.

The most valuable thing you can give your superfans is **access and noticing them.** The privilege of replying to their comments, sending a voicenote DM, taking a photo with them or **appreciating their presence** means everything to a superfan.

STEP TWO - SIMILAR TASTE TO YOUR SUPERFANS

With your superfan in mind, who do they go to gigs with or discuss their top artists with?

Tap into the lives of your fans to see who else they know that loves similar music.

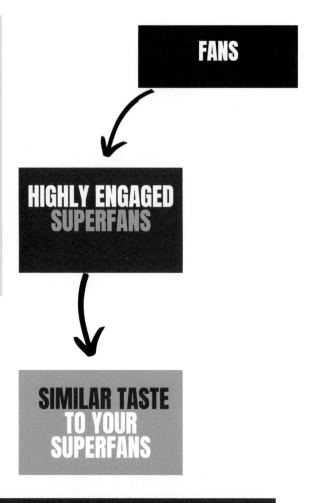

This isn't an excuse to stalk anyone but rather a Six Degree Of Separation stretch to work out the best friends that people connect with on social media and in real life.

Let me show you an incredible way to discover **who likes similar music as you.** Open up <u>any Instagram post</u> either from a celebrity or an actual friend and click on the number of Likes.

The list will show you at the top who you already follow i.e. people you know who like the same music as you.

In exactly the same way, this concept applies to comments and when you click to view all comments the top comments sort by:

a) most liked comment
b) verified users
c) people you know
d) all comments afterwards.

Until now we have talked about your **active fans** who are on the look out for new music because they are highly engaged and on the hunt for fresh sounds and great content.

But what about the **passive fans**? The ones who don't choose to go out and find new music, they wait for it to be discovered and recommended to them via playlists, radio presenters or other music tastemaker friends recommending to them?

By moving away from the mindset of how many followers you have, we start to transition to think about **how many people are paying attention to you right now?**

We all gain and lose followers everyday, so how can we attract some of those audiences back to consume our content?

STEP THREE - FANS WHO HAVE FORGOTTEN ABOUT YOU

Can you think of any usernames of people who <u>used to</u> Like all your posts but hardly show up anymore?

Maybe they **unfollowed** you? Have you checked up on them recently?

Either way, let's attract them back to your brand!

Over time, if you <u>do not</u> **create the type of content** that your perfect fans enjoy seeing, they will move away supporting you.

- Could listeners no longer identify or engage with your topics?

- Did they get fed up of your promotional tone of voice when marketing?

- Has their taste in music shifted to new genres?

STEP FOUR - FANS WHO HAVE NEVER HEARD ABOUT YOU

By creating the right type of content for X's and O's for the sub-audiences in this book, YOU will become suggested by the algorithm and attract new eyeballs daily without doing anything.

You can't control this step except for staying disciplined and make everything you post, speak to the audience in the best possible way.

Once you do have the attention of a small community, what you do with it is up to YOU. My advice would be to give, give, give, then ask: ***"I'm thinking of creating X, what would you like me to create next?"***

CHAPTER FOUR:
CREATING UNIGNORABLE CONTENT

Until now we have only focused on <u>identifying</u> your X's and O's. In this next section we will dive into **what content to create** to attract them to follow your journey.

It is my fundamental belief that musicians struggle to grow a fanbase because they WAIT for opportunities where content could appear, instead of **consciously deciding to CREATE content.**

From this moment onwards, I want you to...

THINK ABOUT YOUR CONTENT AS THE BEST NEW SHOW ON NETFLIX.

As each episode unfolds, you learn more about the character and the backing story throughout all of the highs and lows they experience.

Imagine if the first episode of a series opened up with the finale, without sharing any context to the character arc or the storyline? You'd probably hate it.

That's what it feels like when musicians **release a single WITHOUT explaining the narrative** what the song is about.

What if each episode ended abruptly without a cliffhanger or conclusion? Or what if the programme never informed you when the next episode or season would air?

This is what happens when musicians **run out of content** and disappear into ghost mode after releasing music. They don't give the audience a satisfactory "finale" to the run of content before ramping up curiosity for the next "season" of album promotion.

In my experience, most musicians don't consciously think about the fan experience of what it feels like to consume their content! They focus too much on how they look, **not what they have to say.**

Audiences repeat the content they enjoy most so it's in your best interest to make your show **UNMISSABLE!**

We want to captivate the hearts and minds of our audience by focusing our marketing in two clear areas:

CREATE SPECIFIC CONTENT FOR THE X'S (OTHER MUSICIANS)

AND CREATE SPECIFIC CONTENT FOR THE O'S (THE FANS)

THINK ABOUT YOUR CONTENT AS THE BEST NEW SERIES ON NETFLIX!

AUDIENCES REPEAT THE CONTENT THEY ENJOY MOST

To rebuild your entire posting strategy, we have to unlearn any preconceptions about planning social media content.

You see, because there are **TWO** types of fans **(X's and O's)** we need to define **TWO** different content strategies.

Think about what you post on social media right now. Reflecting on what you have now learnt, would you say that your content is directed at:

A) X'S (OTHER MUSICIANS)
B) O'S (FANS)
C) NOT SPECIFIC ENOUGH TO A TARGET AUDIENCE
D) BOTH AS TWO DIFFERENT CONTENT STREAMS!

Be honest, there's no shame if you chose **B)** or **C)** because this next section is entirely designed to give you clarity how you can plan two different approaches to create content for X's and separately for O's.

CHAPTER FIVE:
YOUR NEW SOCIAL MEDIA STRATEGY

In my years of experience, anything that artists need to post on social media to market their music can be organised into **4 main buckets to identify the purpose** of the message.

TO ENTERTAIN	TO EDUCATE	TO ENGAGE	TO EXCITE

Let's start with a quick definition of each objective in social media terms.

ENTERTAINMENT POSTS

Making your audience smile or laugh is an easy method to capture their interest. When fans find content fun or worth watching, they keep coming back for more. e.g. comedian Munya Chawawa.

EDUCATION POSTS

Teaching a skill or adding informative value to your audiences helps them save your content for future reference or recommend you to other people.

ENAGEMENT POSTS

Asking questions to your audience invites them to share their opinions and thoughts with you. Talk TO your community instead of AT them.

EXCITEMENT POSTS

Ramp up hype and anticipation before you share new music or a big announcement. If you show passion about a subject, the audience will become excited too.

Once you do begin posting in this way and take your audience on a journey through being entertained, educated, engaged and excited they will be ready to become superfans.

It takes time but with the right amount of feel-good energy from your content whilst learning new skills and getting access to talk to your as an artist; your fans will pay attention to your every move.

We're about to break down how these **4 types of posts** can be used differently to create **Recurring Content formats** (repeatable frameworks) to do the same idea over again with different songs and create content for fans and other musicians.

REPEATABLE FORMAT #1 - SONG PERFORMANCE

Showcasing your skill as a singer, rapper, producer or DJ is critical to ENTERTAIN your audience. It is your duty as an artist to **perform** your art.

The question is, how can you make **two different versions of the same performance to entertain** X's (other artists) and O's (the fans)?

PERFORMING IDEAS

- Acoustic Covers
- Remixes
- Freestyle Rapping
- Playing an instrument
- DJ transitions
- Radio show snippets

FOR THE X'S

- Show advanced techniques that other musicians would notice. e.g. DJ scratching

- Playing challenging songs that test the vocal range or ability of the musician.
- e.g. rapping double-time

- Performing at a well known location or venue
- e.g. Spotify Studios

FOR THE O'S

- Perform your own lyrics over Trending or Throwback Instrumentals from other artists.

- Leak your own song and perform it (without telling anyone) it's your next single.

- Add additional music instrumentation on top of a hit song e.g add a saxophone solo or extra drums

PERFORMANCE TITLE SUGGESTIONS

1. If I Performed **SONG NAME** As A **GENRE** Track

2. If I Had A Verse On **ARTIST NAME'S** Song

3. What **ARTIST NAME** Would Sound Like With **ARTIST NAME**

4. Freestyling Over **ARTIST NAME'S 'SONG NAME'**

5. **X** Different Styles Of **GENRE** In 30 Seconds

6. Performing **SONG NAME** If I Were **ARTIST NAME**

7. Writing My Own Lyrics To **ARTIST NAME'S 'SONG NAME'**

WHY THIS STRATEGY WORKS

CATEGORY ONE - ORIGINAL WORDS, YOUR PRODUCTION

Choosing a familiar set of lyrics allows the audience to pay attention to the difference in production and notice the beat difference. This helps your trademark style of beatmaking stand out.

CATEGORY TWO - YOUR WORDS, SOMEONE'S BEAT

Show your songwriting ability by singing or rapping on an iconic instrumental, but you perform with your own words and shine as a talented songwriter or lyricist.

CATEGORY THREE - MIX TWO SONGS CREATIVELY

This method can apply to DJs, Producers or Singers who can add lyrics from Song A to the beat of Song B.

By using the original Song A lyrics, fans will be amazed at the creativity and it could potentially go viral.

REPEATABLE FORMAT #2 - SONG TUTORIAL

Passing on the gems you gained from experience to the next generation is valuable to inspire others who dream of becoming an artist.

You don't have to be a world expert to teach simple tricks, you just have to be willing to share what you already know.

TUTORIAL IDEAS

- Beat production breakdowns
- Songwriting Explanations
- Vocal Excercises
- DJ routine demonstrations
- Performance warm ups
- Travelling tips

FOR THE X'S

- Show the different segments of your song as the drums, synths, bass etc.

- Explain how you protect your voice before and after a studio session.

- Breakdown the process of writing lyrics to an instrumental.

- Teach a beginner artist how to use the software or hardware.

FOR THE O'S

- Decoding what your song means, one line at a time.

- Genius style videos to dissect your song title.

- Instructions how to follow a dance or trend for this song.

- Hacks for packing lots of equipment whilst travelling to sessions, rehearsal and shows.

TUTORIAL TITLE SUGGESTIONS

1. How I Learnt To **SKILL NAME** In **TIME DURATION**

2. Here's A Hack To **SKILL RESULT** Using **INSTRUMENT NAME**

3. How I Warm Up For A Performance As **SINGER / DJ**

4. What I Learned From **BIG MISTAKE**

5. If You Struggle With **TOUGH SKILL**, Try This...

6. How To Play My Song **YOUR SONG TITLE**

7. Breaking Down How I Made **YOUR SONG TITLE**

WHY THIS STRATEGY WORKS

CATEGORY ONE - HOW I LEARNED A,B,C

Whatever level of skill you reach as an artist, the next generation on the come up will want to learn the techniques you use in your music. Teach them and you will build a community of **X's (other musicians).**

CATEGORY TWO - PROBLEM AND SOLUTION

Educating others how to solve problems helps them see you as a authority figure in the space that they will share your content and recommend you to others.

CATEGORY THREE - BREAKDOWN YOUR SONGS

This method is goldust because it simultaneously encourages artists to want to remix your song after hearing the components as drums, synths, vocals etc but also they become familar with your songs and will want to listen as fans.

REPEATABLE FORMAT #3 - POLL OR Q&A

One of the most important things your audience want, is **access to you**. Audiences get excited when you take the time out of your busy day to **notice them** and individually reply to their comment, Story reply, Question Sticker, Poll or Inbox Message.

By knowing this, you can ask the right questions that get your audience to share answers and interact with you (which creates more submissions).

POLL OR Q&A IDEAS

- Genre comparisons
- Musical equipment reviews
- Technique discussions
- Favourite artist rankings
- Non-musical topics
- Next song to release

FOR THE X'S

- Ask for suggestions on the best plugins or tools.

- If you are thinking of investing in some gear, survey your community to ask which of your options is best.

- Share a book or album most artists have read and give a controversial opinion about the best chapter or line.

FOR THE O'S

- Rank your favourite albums or artists and get the audience to vote if they agree.

- Share snippets or titles of new musical ideas and ask which one should be the next release.

- Let your audience vote on your trainer choices for a music video or show.

- Ask what podcasts, interviews or albums are your fans are listening to.

POLL / Q&A TITLE SUGGESTIONS

1. What's The Best **ITEM NAME** To Buy Under **£XX?**

2. Who's The Best Podcaster To Listen To About **TOPIC**?

3. Where is the Best **PLACE** To Visit In **LOCATION**?

4. Who Can Recommend A Must-See **GENRE** Gig In **LOCATION**?

5. Which **GENRE** Songs Shall I Perform Next Week?

6. How Would You Rank ARTIST'S Albums Of All Time?

7. Which **GENRE** Artists Make The Greatest Of All Time List?

WHY THIS STRATEGY WORKS

CATEGORY ONE - CONTENT RECOMMENDATIONS

Asking your followers for their input on choosing what to listen to or read helps them feel comfortable enough to share their opinions with you. This communication building is the first step to encourage your audience to engage with your music in the future.

CATEGORY TWO - MUST SEE PLACES AND EXPERIENCES

Sourcing recommended places or events to visit helps create opportunities to meet your audience. Alternatively, if they share the best itinerary of things to do, you'll build trust by visiting and capturing content in that location.

CATEGORY THREE - RANKING TIMELESS MUSIC

This controversial method is a quick way to spike comments by playing on people's strong opinions. Someone may not comment on your music but hip-hop or R&B debates will endlessly create interaction.

REPEATABLE FORMAT #4 - DAY IN THE LIFE REEL

Now that you've worked out the three recurring formats that you need to use, it's finally time to excite your fans. You can do this by creating short montage day in the life content which will perfectly fit Reels or TikTok.

You can combine 3 second videos with timelapses and add sounds or songs from the Instagram or TikTok Audio Library (not using the sound of the actual videos you filmed).

REEL IDEAS

- Concert footage with voiceover
- Day In The Studio
- Zoom and In-Person Meetings
- Campaign Planning
- Industry Events and Gigs

FOR THE X'S

- Travelling from your home to the studio and then meeting other artists.

- Working out early in the morning then heading to a meeting.

- Non-stop Zoom calls or meetings as a timelapse

- Montage of no-audio footage of you in the recording booth

FOR THE O'S

- Wrap Up Video the day after a gig showing backstage moments.

- Funny moments with artist friends like ordering food or playing video games.

- Jam sessions in your bedroom or rehearsal room showing the BTS of making TikToks or performance videos.

- What makes you happy other than music to show your passions and interests.

I want you to think of yourself as the **CEO behind your own hustle**, not just a vehicle to promote content when you have something to share.

Empower yourself to show what's in progress behind the scenes without announcing any specific details at all.

You don't need to say this song is your next single.
You don't need to unveil the release date.
You don't need to share whom else collaborated on the song.

In the past 6 months of writing this ebook, every guest podcast I've spoken on, every YouTube video I filmed, every post was all geared up to tease the principles you are reading right now.

This is how you play chess with your audience and drop Easter Egg clues across the lifespan of a project.

Surprisingly, Taylor Swift does this really well by leaving small hints in the tiny corners of her artwork that unveil the initials of future song titles.

Get comfortable, being uncomfortable and set up a camera to capture you on a Zoom call, take a photo after a meeting, film some content whilst eating fast food on a break in the studio.

Be a boss who **treats the fans to sneak previews of your hustle every single day.** Most likely, artists are grinding every single day on their craft. But they are not showing the determination by taking content.

CHAPTER SIX:
DUPLICATE THEN STAGGER

Wait! Before you start panicking and wondering if this strategy is for **Facebook, Instagram, TikTok or YouTube**... bear with me.

The final mystery I bet you must be thinking by now is: "hold up which channel am I supposed to put this content on? Is this for **Reels, Stories or for the Feed**?? What about **YouTube Shorts or TikTok?**

Right now, it's more important to visualise **where** your audience naturally hang out. If everybody you know is saying how much time they waste scrolling on TikTok, you need to be there showing up when they are scrolling.

If nobody in your friends list actively posts on Facebook anymore, you can safely say that's not the right channel for you at this moment.

Whichever channels you choose to activate these strategies on, I want to **duplicate and then stagger,** so you need to post **identical content with identical captions** on your:

- Instagram Feed
- Facebook Profile
- Facebook Page
- Twitter feed
- TikTok channel
- YouTube Shorts

That's <u>not</u> a sustainable long-term strategy but it does get you active across all channels quick to test and learn what works.

By **measuring the analytics daily for the first 4 weeks** consistently, you can establish which channels was best and name that as your primary platform to upload content there first.

Then two days later, you can stagger content back onto all the other places with a **modified caption**. This trains your audience to realise that they have to follow you on the primary platform to **see the content first** and in its best form.

Copy and pasting captions forever, won't be effective because it removes the incentive for fans to follow you on all platforms. If they have seen your Twitter, they don't need you on Instagram for example!

Although everyone is talking about Instagram Reels in 2021, don't get too attached to this format because the game is always changing and I never want to pigeonhole you into a format that's only temporary. I'm building you up to survive a marathon not a 100 metre sprint.

WHAT TO DO NEXT?

From the bottom of my heart, I hope this book **changes your life** and you apply these techniques to rebirth your social media habits, identity, content strategy, repeatable formats and post intentions.

The most rewarding feeling in the world would be to receive an Inbox Message from you telling me you've hit a new follow milestone or you've never, ever had so many comments before!

My first suggestion would be to write out the titles of 100 Songs you want to perform (Repeatable Format #1) and 100 Techniques you want to teach (Repeatable Format #2).

Then create one of each video type per week and you've planned almost **2 YEARS worth of content** (52 Weeks In A year, 2 Videos A Week).

I can promise you two phases will happen as you start this journey. Firstly that your Likes, Comments, Views, Shares will accelerate for the initial 2-3 Videos.

The second phase is that YOU need to stop yourself from slipping backwards into old habits. Remember, **replace promotion with emotion** and stop the dysfunctional tactics you used to do without any success to attract interaction.

In this part of your content journey it's highly likely that your engagement **will slow down** as you change the effort level you put into the marketing and rollout of your content.

Don't give up though, as long as <u>one person</u> finds your content entertaining, educating, engaging or exciting then you can consider it a success.

The only way to guarantee zero eyeballs is by <u>not posting</u> at all. You control the journey from this point.

Promise yourself, no weeks off.
No excuses about bad time management to film and edit.
No rushing to ***"just get it out there"***
No impulse selfies ***"because you haven't posted in a while"***
No comparisons against other creators with more views.
No sense of defeat from not growing fast enough.

Begin today, tomorrow or next week... but at least begin and create content that **targets both X's and O's.**

You've learnt who they are and you've discovered how to target them.

Congratulations, you're ready!

But if you do decide you want more help, reach out to us here and let's have a chat:

hello@allabouthelping.co.uk

That's the end of your training, I can't wait to see what you do next.

Ayaz Aftab Hussain

Printed in Great Britain
by Amazon

44011638R00034